GRAPHIC PREHISTORIC ANIMALS

WOOLLY MAMMOTH

MAMMUTHUS

ILLUSTRATED BY ALESSANDRO POLUZZI

A+

Smart Apple Media

Published by Smart Apple Media, an imprint of Black Rabbit Books
P.O. Box 3263, Mankato, Minnesota 56002
www.blackrabbitbooks.com

Produced by David West ☖☖ Children's Books
6 Princeton Court, 55 Felsham Road, London SW15 1AZ

Designed and written by Gary Jeffrey

Copyright © 2017 David West Children's Books

Library of Congress Cataloging-in-Publication Data

Names: Jeffrey, Gary, author. | Poluzzi, Alessandro, illustrator.
Title: Woolly mammoth / written by Gary Jeffrey ; illustrated by Alessandro
    Poluzzi.
Description: Mankato, Minnesota : Smart Apple Media, [2017] | Series: Graphic prehistoric animals | Audience: K to grade 3._ | Includes index.
Identifiers: LCCN 2015036959| ISBN 9781625884145 (library binding) | ISBN 9781625884305 (ebook)
Subjects: LCSH: Woolly mammoth–Juvenile literature. | Woolly mammoth—Comic books, strips, etc. | Mammals, Fossil–Juvenile literature. | Mammals,
    Fossil–Comic books, strips, etc. | CYAC: Prehistoric animals. | LCGFT:
    Graphic novels.
Classification: LCC QE882.P8 W46 2017 | DDC 569.67–dc23
LC record available at http://lccn.loc.gov/2015036959

Printed in China
CPSIA compliance information: DWCB16CP
010116

9 8 7 6 5 4 3 2 1

CONTENTS

WHAT IS A WOOLLY MAMMOTH?

MAMMUTHUS IS THE SCIENTIFIC NAME FOR ALL MAMMOTHS

The woolly mammoth lived around 200,000 to 4,000 years ago, during the **Pleistocene** and **Holocene periods**. **Fossils** and **mummies** of its skeleton have been found in North America, Northern Europe, and Asia (see page 22).

It had big teeth—four **molars** and two tusks. The tusks curved inward to help balance their weight.

Its tusks were used to clear away snow from the ground to feed, to rub bark from trees, and to fend off **predators**.

It used its tusks in fights with rival males.

It stored a hump of fat on its shoulders to help it survive the lean winters.

It had two "fingertips" at the end of its trunk that could pluck grass and plants.

MAMMUTHUS *PRIMIGENIUS* (FIRST MAMMOTH) MEASURED UP TO 11 FEET (3.4 M) HIGH AND WEIGHED 6 TONS (5,443 KG). THE LARGEST TUSKS WERE 14 FEET (4.3 M) LONG.

Its outer fur was 3 feet (1 m) long. Under that was a shorter coat, and beneath its skin, there was a 4-inch (10-cm) layer of fat.

This would be a woolly mammoth and you.

MAMMOTH FACTS

Woolly mammoths lived during the last two ice ages. They were similar to Asian elephants, but they had adapted to the cold. They were covered with brown fur and were bulked out with fat. Both sexes of mammoths evolved long tusks to help them cope with their frozen world and with the large predators that hunted them. Unlike modern-day elephants, they had small ears and short tails to minimize heat loss and frostbite. The shape of their trunk tips enabled them to pluck up the plants that grew on the **steppe**.

Adult woolly mammoths had to eat 500 pounds (226 kg) of food each day. Their molars had hardened ridges to grind down tough plant stalks and bark. They grew new molars six times throughout their lives. By cutting a section through a tusk, scientists can age mammoths by counting growth rings. The oldest ones lived to be 60.

a mammoth molar

Like elephants today, it is believed that mammoths formed social herds of females, led by an older matriarch. The females would be sought out by lone males during breeding season.

WOOLLY MAMMOTHS ON THE GRASSLANDS OF ANCIENT EUROPE

WINTER IN NORTHERN EUROPE, 150,000 YEARS AGO

FOR MORE THAN SIX WEEKS, A HERD OF WOOLLY MAMMOTHS HAS BEEN TRAVELING FROM THE FROZEN NORTH, HEADING TOWARD THE MILDER GRASSLANDS OF THE SOUTHWEST.

THE MAMMOTHS BRAVED RAVENING SCIMITAR CATS...

...AND TERRIBLE STORMS.

UNLIKE IN THE NORTH, THE GROUND HERE IS NOT FROZEN HARD. THE MATRIARCH OF THE HERD CAN USE HER TRUNK TO PULL UP A BUNCH OF TASTY GROUND PLANTS.

SHE IS ON HER SIXTH, AND FINAL, SET OF TEETH. THEY ACT LIKE GRINDING PLATES TO BREAK UP VEGETATION.

WHEN THESE LAST TEETH ARE WORN DOWN, HER LIFE WILL BE AT AN END. BUT SHE IS ONLY 50 YEARS OLD, AND THEY WILL LAST FOR SOME YEARS YET.

THE MAMMOTHS SHARE THE GRASSLANDS WITH OTHER GRAZERS— ANCIENT HORSES AND REINDEER, HAIRY MUSK OX, AND WOOLLY RHINO.

SUCH PLENTIFUL PREY ATTRACTS PREDATORS TOO.

AS IT HEADS TOWARD THE RIVER, THE HERD PASSES CAVE LIONS FEASTING.

THE LIONS WILL EAT THEIR FILL BEFORE RETURNING TO THEIR HOMES IN THE ROCKY HILLSIDES TO SLEEP.

NEARBY, SPOTTED HYENAS WAIT FOR THEIR TURN AT THE LEFTOVERS, DARING EACH OTHER TO GET CLOSE ENOUGH TO GRAB A SNACK.

THE MATRIARCH LEADS THE HERD ACROSS THE NARROWEST PART OF THE RIVER.

THE CALF GRASPS HER MOTHER'S TAIL. HER FEET BARELY TOUCH THE BOTTOM.

THE HERD MUST KEEP MOVING TO FRESH PASTURES. THE MAMMOTHS EAT CONSTANTLY FOR 20 HOURS AT A TIME.

THEY HEAD TOWARD A LINE OF ROCKY CLIFFS WHERE THIN TRAILS OF SMOKE ARE RISING INTO THE SKY.

THEY HAVE STRAYED INTO THE TERRITORY OF THE MOST DANGEROUS PREDATOR OF ALL.

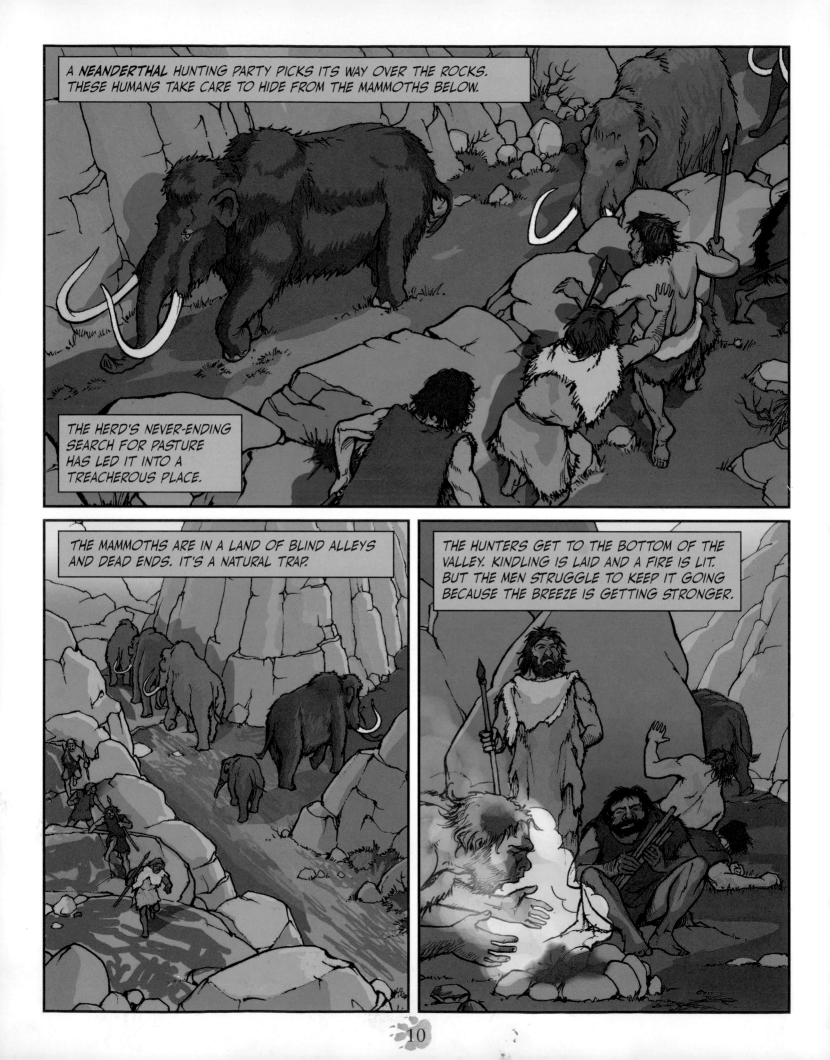

A **NEANDERTHAL** HUNTING PARTY PICKS ITS WAY OVER THE ROCKS. THESE HUMANS TAKE CARE TO HIDE FROM THE MAMMOTHS BELOW.

THE HERD'S NEVER-ENDING SEARCH FOR PASTURE HAS LED IT INTO A TREACHEROUS PLACE.

THE MAMMOTHS ARE IN A LAND OF BLIND ALLEYS AND DEAD ENDS. IT'S A NATURAL TRAP.

THE HUNTERS GET TO THE BOTTOM OF THE VALLEY. KINDLING IS LAID AND A FIRE IS LIT. BUT THE MEN STRUGGLE TO KEEP IT GOING BECAUSE THE BREEZE IS GETTING STRONGER.

THE LEADER LOOKS NORTH TOWARD THE DIRECTION OF THE WIND.

THE DISTANT LINE OF MOUNTAINS HAS DISAPPEARED. A DUST STORM IS HEADING THEIR WAY.

BUT THE MEN HAVE TO HUNT. THE MAMMOTHS ARE EXACTLY WHERE THEY WANT THEM. THIS MAY BE THEIR ONLY CHANCE FOR MONTHS.

IN CAVES ON THE OTHER SIDE OF THE HILL, THE HUNTERS' FAMILIES PREPARE FIRES FOR COOKING AND SHARPEN THEIR CUTTING TOOLS —HOPEFUL THAT THEY WILL SOON BE NEEDED.

MEANWHILE, THE CALF FOLLOWS THE MATRIARCH INTO A SIDE CANYON.

THE CALF STOPS, STARTLED BY A GOLDEN EAGLE AS IT CAPTURES A MOUNTAIN HARE.

THE MATRIARCH HAS MOVED ON WITHOUT HER. THE CALF SMELLS THE AIR FOR THE SCENT OF THE HERD.

SNIFF SNIFF

SHE CATCHES THE HERD'S SCENT— AND AN UNFAMILIAR SMELL TOO.

THE GROUND GIVES LITTLE MOVEMENTS UNDER HER SENSITIVE FEET. IT'S THE SOUND OF SMALLER ANIMALS MOVING AROUND.

A STRANGE, PIGLIKE SMELL...

SPOOKED, SHE RUNS OUT OF THE CANYON TO FOLLOW THE SCENT OF THE HERD. THE HUNTING PARTY EMERGES FROM THE ROCKS BEHIND HER.

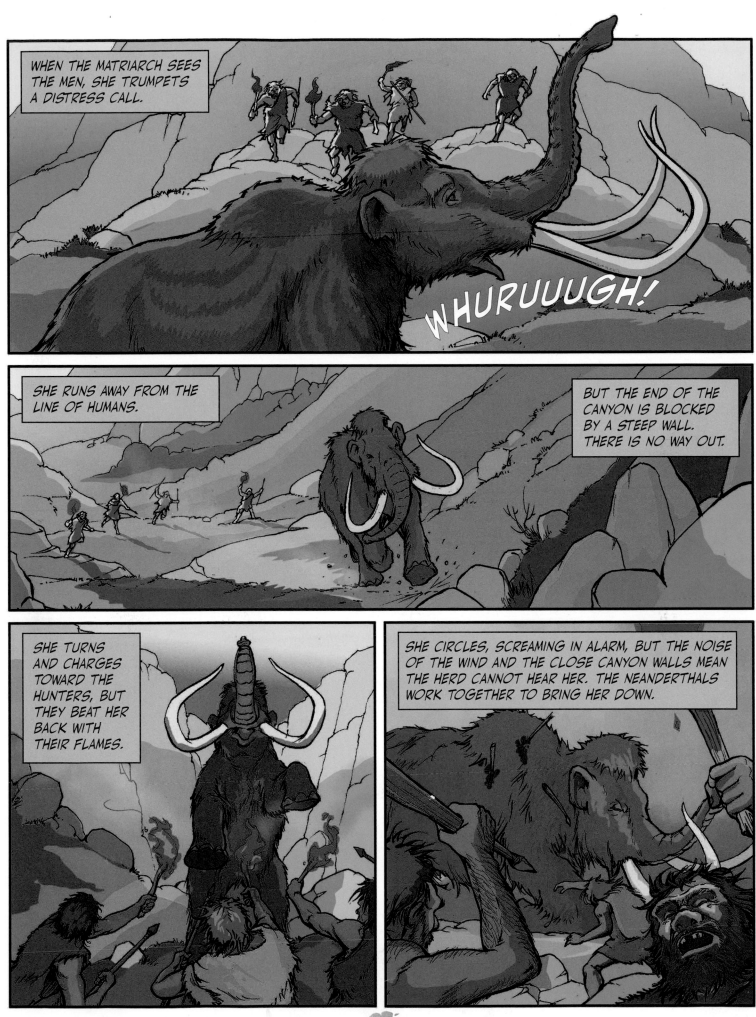

WHEN THE MATRIARCH SEES THE MEN, SHE TRUMPETS A DISTRESS CALL.

WHURUUUGH!

SHE RUNS AWAY FROM THE LINE OF HUMANS.

BUT THE END OF THE CANYON IS BLOCKED BY A STEEP WALL. THERE IS NO WAY OUT.

SHE TURNS AND CHARGES TOWARD THE HUNTERS, BUT THEY BEAT HER BACK WITH THEIR FLAMES.

SHE CIRCLES, SCREAMING IN ALARM, BUT THE NOISE OF THE WIND AND THE CLOSE CANYON WALLS MEAN THE HERD CANNOT HEAR HER. THE NEANDERTHALS WORK TOGETHER TO BRING HER DOWN.

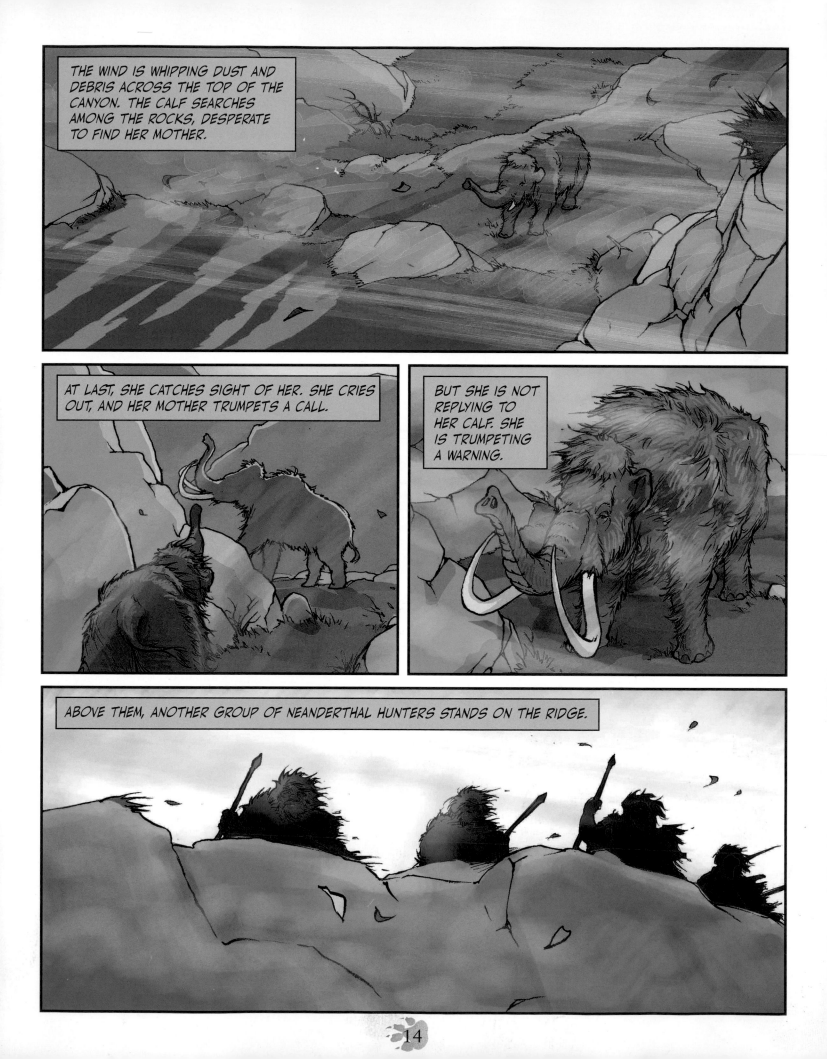

THE WIND IS WHIPPING DUST AND DEBRIS ACROSS THE TOP OF THE CANYON. THE CALF SEARCHES AMONG THE ROCKS, DESPERATE TO FIND HER MOTHER.

AT LAST, SHE CATCHES SIGHT OF HER. SHE CRIES OUT, AND HER MOTHER TRUMPETS A CALL.

BUT SHE IS NOT REPLYING TO HER CALF. SHE IS TRUMPETING A WARNING.

ABOVE THEM, ANOTHER GROUP OF NEANDERTHAL HUNTERS STANDS ON THE RIDGE.

THE DUST STORM BREAKS OVER THE PLAIN, SENDING THE GRAZERS RUNNING FOR COVER. A WATER SPOUT RISES FROM THE RIVER.

ON THE RIDGE, THE HUNTERS TURN AWAY TO SEEK SHELTER AS THE STORM RACES IN.

THE STORM IS ON TOP OF THEM. THE CALF CAN FEEL HER BODY BEING LIFTED SLIGHTLY FROM THE GROUND BY THE FORCE OF THE WIND. THE AIR SWIRLS WITH DEBRIS. THE HOWLING WIND IS DEAFENING. DUST STINGS HER EYES.

THE CALF IS RUNNING BLIND.

THE WIND FINALLY WEAKENS. THE CALF HAS MANAGED TO STAY ON HER FEET. THROUGH THE DUST SWIRL, SHE MAKES OUT A FAMILIAR HUMPED SHAPE AND HEADS TOWARD IT.

THE CALF RAISES HER TRUNK TO GREET THE OTHER MAMMOTH...

BWURUUUUGH!

...BUT IT IS A LONE NEANDERTHAL HUNTER, SHELTERING FROM THE STORM. THE HUNTER IS STARTLED BY THE SIGHT OF THE MAMMOTH.

QUICKLY HE GATHERS HIS WITS, CASTS HIS FUR CLOAK ASIDE, AND RAISES HIS FLINT-TIPPED SPEAR. IF HE CAN JUST DISABLE THE CALF, HE WILL BE ABLE TO CALL TO THE OTHERS TO HELP HIM KILL IT.

THE HUNTER HOLDS HIS SPEAR IN READINESS, WAITING TO SEE WHICH WAY THE MAMMOTH WILL GO.

AT THAT MOMENT THERE IS A FLASH OF MOVEMENT IN THE CORNER OF HIS EYE. HE TURNS HIS HEAD TO SEE WHAT'S THERE.

RAAAAAAH

A CAVE LION POUNCES, KNOCKING THE NEANDERTHAL OFF HIS FEET.

THE LION HAD BEEN PROWLING THE CAVES, LOOKING FOR UNGUARDED BEAR CUBS. THIS PREY IS A LUCKY PRIZE FOR THE CAT, SINCE HUMANS DO NOT USUALLY TRAVEL ALONE.

HE QUICKLY KILLS THE MAN WITH A POWERFUL BITE TO THE THROAT.

WHILE THE CAVE LION IS BUSY FEEDING, THE MAMMOTH CALF MAKES HER ESCAPE.

SHE RACES ALONG, TRYING TO PICK UP A TRACE OF THE HERD'S SCENT.

BUT SHE IS STILL IN DANGER. LIKE HUMANS, CAVE LIONS RARELY HUNT ALONE.

THE CALF HALTS SUDDENLY AT THE EDGE OF A CLIFF. OFF THE CLIFF, THERE'S A STEEP DROP TO BOULDERS AND A STREAM BELOW.

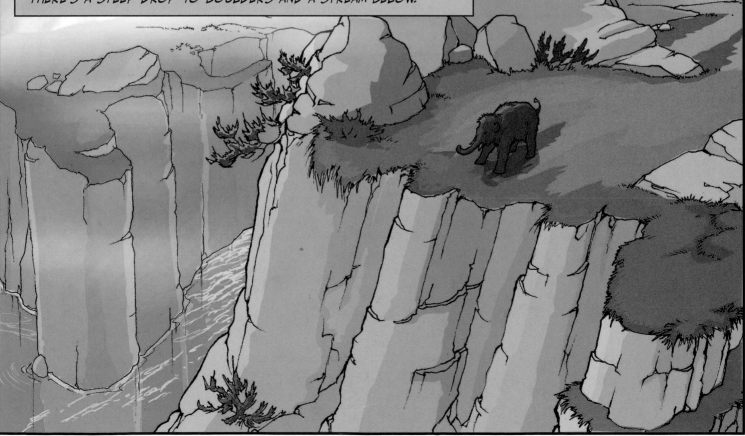

A CAVE LIONESS IS ON A ROCK ABOVE THE CALF, AND SHE'S ABOUT TO POUNCE.

THE CALF IS TRAPPED. SHE CRIES OUT LOUDLY, BUT WHO WILL HEAR HER? IT SEEMS A LIFETIME HAS PASSED SINCE SHE LAST SAW HER HERD.

GRAAAAR

BWURUUUUGH!

THE CAVE LIONESS LEAPS TOWARD THE CALF'S BACK.

BUT A HARD, WHITE TUSK IS THRUST IN HER WAY.

CLOMP

THE CALF'S MOTHER HAS FINALLY HEARD THE CALF'S CRIES OF DISTRESS AND HAS RACED TO PROTECT HER. THE LIONESS DANGLES FROM HER TUSK AND TRIES TO CLAW AT THE MAMMOTH'S FACE, BUT SHE CAN'T REACH IT.

20

THE MOTHER TOSSES THE BIG CAT INTO THE RAVINE.

THE HERD MOVES ON. THEY ALL SURVIVED EXCEPT FOR THE MATRIARCH, THAT BECAME FOOD FOR THE CAVE PEOPLE.

IN THE SPRING, THE MAMMOTHS WILL MAKE THEIR WAY BACK TO THEIR SUMMER FEEDING GROUNDS IN THE FROZEN NORTH. THEY WILL BE WELL AWAY FROM THE THREAT OF MAN, UNTIL WINTER BLIZZARDS ONCE AGAIN DRIVE THEM TO MAKE THE DANGEROUS JOURNEY SOUTH.

BRUUUGH!

FOSSIL FINDS

WE CAN GET A GOOD IDEA OF WHAT **ANCIENT ANIMALS** MAY HAVE LOOKED LIKE FROM THEIR FOSSILS. FOSSILS ARE FORMED WHEN THE HARD PARTS OF AN ANIMAL OR PLANT BECOME BURIED AND THEN TURN TO ROCK OVER MILLIONS OF YEARS.

Woolly mammoth fossils have been found from North America to China and even under the North Sea (which was dry land during the coldest ice ages). Mammoth remains were sought by ancient people long before today's **paleontologists**. The fossilized ivory "tusks" were valued by them.

Some mammoths have been found deep frozen in **permafrost** with mummified flesh, skin, fur, and even the contents of their stomachs.

"Dima" is a seven-month-old frozen mammoth who was found in Siberia.

During the last two ice ages, woolly mammoths co-existed with Neanderthals and **Cro-Magnon** humans. We know this from finding bones that show cuts, or butchering marks, at human sites. Early humans also depicted mammoths in cave art and on small stone carvings. In Siberia they used mammoth bones, tusks, and skins to build shelters.

"Oscar" is the largest fossil woolly mammoth.

ANIMAL GALLERY

All of these **animals** appear in the story.

mountain hare

Lepus timidus
Length: 26 inches (66 cm)
A typical hare adapted to harsh polar and **tundra** *habitats. Still living.*

golden eagle

Aquila chrysaetos
Wingspan: 7.8 ft (2.4 m)
A majestic bird of prey with massive talons. It is the most widespread modern-day eagle.

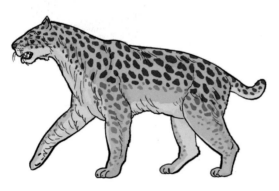

scimitar cat

Homotherium
Length: 5.5 ft (1.7 m)
A lion-sized cat that ran and hunted like a cheetah and had two extra-large **canine** *teeth.*

Neanderthal

Homo neanderthalensis
Height: up to 5.5 ft (1.7 m)
A type of early human that made fire, stone tools, and hunted. They became extinct about 40,000 years ago.

woolly rhinoceros

Coelodonta antiquitatis
Length: 10–12.5 ft (3–3.8 m)
Similar to today's African rhino but it was adapted to the cold.

musk ox

Ovibos moschatus
Length: 4.4–8.2ft (1.3–2.5 m)
A large-headed oxen with a heavy coat that still exists.

cave lion

Panthera leo spelaea
Length: 7 ft (2.1 m)
One of the largest lions that ever lived. May have been patterned.

GLOSSARY

canine a pointed tooth used by meat-eating animals for tearing flesh

Cro-Magnon the earliest type of modern humans who appeared 35,000 years ago

fossils the remains of a dead animal or plant that have turned to rock

Holocene period the time from 10,000 years ago to the present day

molars cheek teeth for chewing

mummies well-preserved, dried out bodies or remains of dead animals

Neanderthal an extinct species of human

paleontologists scientists who study fossils

permafrost a thick layer of undersoil that stays frozen all year

Pleistocene period the time between 1,640,000 to 10,000 years ago, marked by a series of great ice ages

predators animals that naturally prey on others for food

ravening attacking through extreme hunger

steppe a large area of flat unforested grassland

tundra vast flat treeless grasslands on permafrost

INDEX